EIGHTH NOTE ♪ PUBLICATIONS

Canzon per Sonare #4

T0043218

Giovanni Gabrieli
Arranged by David Marlatt

Canzoni were pieces composed for various combinations of instruments and various sizes of ensembles. This particular work was originally for four oboes and four bassoons. The actual instrumentation of many of Giovanni Gabrieli's canzoni is not known, mainly because these pieces were designed for an ensemble of non-specific instruments. They were often performed combining oboes, violins, trumpets, trombones, gambas and many others. The most famous set of Gabrieli canzoni was his *Sacrae symphoniae* (1597). Included in these 16 works is the famous *Sonata piano e forte* which links the canzon and the sonata.

Dynamics and articulations have been added by the arranger and may be altered or ignored.

ISBN: 9781771579193
CATALOG NUMBER: WWE222189

COST: $15.00
DURATION: 2:10

DIFFICULTY RATING: Medium
2 Flutes, 2 Clarinets

www.enpmusic.com

CANZON PER SONARE #4

G. Gabrieli
(1557-1612)
Arranged by David Marlatt

Flute 1

CANZON PER SONARE #4

G. Gabrieli
(1557-1612)
Arranged by David Marlatt

CANZON PER SONARE #4

Flute 2

G. Gabrieli
(1557-1612)
Arranged by David Marlatt

CANZON PER SONARE #4

B♭ Clarinet 1

G. Gabrieli
(1557-1612)
Arranged by David Marlatt